little

prayer
book

49 pocket sized
prayers

Vincent H. Chough

ISBN: 9781718164390

TO WHOM ELSE SHALL YOU GO?

Go to your loving and all-powerful God. He will lift you up and out of the pit of despair. The Lord gives you wings to soar above the chaos of this world. He forgives even your worst moments. Jesus places you upon his throne as a child of God.

CONTENTS

HERE & NOW

You never quite know when your prayers will take effect – or when you'll need to pray. But remember: prayer works right now. First, a change happens in your heart. Just stopping to give God priority shows how much you love and depend on him.

In our busy and hectic lives, a moment or two might be all we can spare sometimes. For those situations – when you need a bit of courage and hope – this little book is your companion.

Each prayer focuses on a different life challenge. I wrote them when I faced difficulty or when I wanted to praise God. Every word you read is saturated with real world prayer. An accompanying Bible passage sheds even more light on the topic. My hope is that the words inspire you to listen to God and to talk to him.

Let your prayer rise up into the wondrous reality of heavenly grace. It all returns to the same purpose: a glorious and intimate relationship with Jesus Christ.

Be abundantly blessed,
Vincent

1 HEAR THE SPIRIT

Do not be conformed to this world but be
transformed by the renewal of your mind, that
you may prove what is the will of God, what is
good and acceptable and perfect.

Romans 12:2

Dear heavenly Father,
Here I am in your presence.
Speak to me Lord.
Fill me with your Spirit.
Give me the gift of hearing and obeying your voice.
Let me be in tune with your Spirit. May I hear his call.
Transform me, my Lord.
Let me not hesitate or be afraid.
For when the Lord speaks, his will must be done.
Let me listen to and trust your voice.
Teach me to depend completely on you.
May I abandon myself, and present myself, as a living
sacrifice to almighty God.
All for the glory and honor of the King of kings.
Accept my prayer, oh loving Father.
In the name of your beloved Son,
Jesus Christ.
Amen.

2 FAMILY

Love is patient and kind; love is not jealous or boastful; it is not arrogant or rude. Love does not insist on its own way; it is not irritable or resentful; it does not rejoice at wrong, but rejoices in the right. Love bears all things, believes all things, hopes all things, endures all things.

1 Corinthians 13:4-7

Oh loving Lord,
Do you see my family?
Do you see how we struggle? How we hurt?
Even each other. Pain going back for generations.
We're not a perfect family that never suffers,
that never bleeds.
So right here, right now, in your presence,
I claim your promises for me and my family.
Make us a family united in **LOVE,**
in Spirit and in Truth.
This can only come by your grace.
Oh loving Lord, pour yourself out upon us.
Wash us clean again. Reach down, restore us.
Through your mercy, through your love,
In Jesus' name,
Amen.

3 OVERWHELMED

The Lord is my light and my salvation;
whom shall I fear?
The Lord is the stronghold of my life;
of whom shall I be afraid?

Wait for the Lord;
be strong, and let your heart take courage;
yea, wait for the Lord!

Psalm 27:1,13

Oh holy Father,
I seek you as I feel completely overwhelmed.
I do not have the time or energy to sustain myself.
Everything tells me there is too much to do.
Won't you help me, oh Lord?
Show me your hand in control of all things.
Let me rest in you.
May I trust that you give me eternal blessings always.
You alone are sovereign. You alone are the Lord.
So I stop at this moment and look for you,
to feel the soft breeze of your merciful love
carrying my worries away.
You transform me. You change my heart.
I rise up strong again, in CHRIST.
I face the world, my path straight and firm,
with faith in your Son Jesus.
In his great name I pray,
Amen.

4 KEEP GOING

"For my Father's will is that everyone who looks to the Son and believes in him shall have eternal life, and I will raise them up at the last day."

John 6:40

Dear holy Father,
The pressure mounts and troubles close in.
I need your grace to return to you.
I don't want to be a hero or the easy way out.
All I want, all I need, is your loving mercy.
I know you never leave me, oh Lord.
Keep me under your wing.
Even if I don't feel you there, at least let me
understand that you *are* there.
Give me the strength to take up my cross
and fight the good fight.
By your grace may I trust in the only one that gives
me truth and clarity – despite the trial and pain.
Fill my soul with the abundant joy that
only your Spirit gives.
For in the Messiah, I find my resurrection.
In Christ almighty, all things are made new.
In Jesus' name,
Amen.

5 LETTER FROM JESUS

Dear beloved child,

I know sometimes you feel troubled. I know you feel weak. I see you at times trembling with fear and confusion about your life. I know you might feel lonely and afraid. So I want to tell you now, my dear child, your suffering reaches my ears and my heart. You may think that I don't hear your cry, but know this: I hear your cry of anguish. I cry with you, and our cry reaches my Father in heaven.

Your pain and suffering never, not for a single instant, go unheard. Every tear and every moment of worry pierces my heart. My heart bleeds from all the sadness you feel.

Know that all your pain I have taken upon myself. Even before it hurt you, it was placed in my wounded side for all eternity. All your suffering, shame and fear I took upon me so that you could be at peace with my Father. I have done this for all humankind. For this my Father lifted me up and glorified me, his Son, above all others. This reason, above all, is why I came. I want to give you the one thing that I am sure will help you in any uncertain moment: my peace. I give you my peace, with nothing held back. I give you the peace that comes only from my Spirit. My Spirit tells you who I am and what I did for you, and all the splendor and majesty of God is found within my peace.

My peace sets you free. Do not fear.

My peace heals you. Be strong

Trust in my peace. Receive my peace.

It is my love poured out for you from before time itself and continuing eternally.

Rest, beloved child, in the loving arms of my peace.

6 NEED FORGIVENESS

*for this is my blood of the covenant,
which is poured out for many for the
forgiveness of sins.*

Matthew 26:28

Dear loving Lord,
When I think of what I've done,
I can hardly even bring myself into your presence.
I hurt myself and others. I have gone against you.
I feel so wretched. It's so hard to pray now.
Will you forgive me? Is it possible?
Let me know, oh Lord, that it's not about me
or my behavior.
It's about your Son taking it all upon him
to redeem me, to purify me.
This is his work alone. This is why he came.
Oh, dear Lord, let it pierce my heart,
and may my heart be changed.
Please forgive me. Please have mercy.
Pour out, **the Blood of Christ** over me.
Cleanse me Jesus,
with your sweet love,
in your holy name,
Amen.

7 PEACE AT HOME

Jesus came and stood among them and said to them, "Peace be with you." When he had said this, he showed them his hands and his side. Then the disciples were glad when they saw the Lord.

John 20:19b-20

Dear loving Lord,
My home needs your peace. My family needs you.
Won't you come to us and set us free?
Pour out your love, pour out your Spirit.
Wash us clean, cover us and protect us.
By the blood of Christ we are cleansed.
From his wounds mercy and peace come forth
to heal the wounds between us.
Let us respect and listen to one another.
Let us love each other.
Begin with me, dear Lord. Change me first.
Give me strength.
Show me how to love more.
Show me how to care more.
Show me how to forgive.
May your Spirit change me while you care for the others. Let me trust in your ways.
They are in your hands, just like me.
In the name of sweet Jesus,
Amen.

8 TRUST

But he said to me, "My grace is sufficient for
you, for my power is made perfect in weakness."
Therefore I will boast all the more gladly about
my weaknesses, so that Christ's power may rest
on me.

2 Corinthians 12:9

Oh heavenly Father
Do you see my struggle?
Do you see how hard it is for me to let go?
Won't you help me Lord?
Let me not be fooled by my lack of trust in you.
Defend me from the enemy who tells me I can do
it all. Or even worse, that there is no hope.
No, I am not alone. A great God stands with me.
Rise up now, oh Lord, rise up!
Cast out the doubt! Strike down my pride!
Your grace alone is more than enough for me.
What more do I need to face this troubled world?
I know my Savior loves me.
He bled and died for me.
The Spirit gives me supernatural gifts
of patience, love and self-control.
May I trust in you, only you, oh loving Lord.
As only you have the Words of Eternal Life.
In Jesus' name,
Amen.

9 SLEEP & REST

Come to me, all who labor and are heavy laden, and I will give you rest. Take my yoke upon you, and learn from me; for I am gentle and lowly in heart, and you will find rest for your souls. For my yoke is easy, and my burden is light.

Matthew 11:28-30

Dear loving God,
I'm so tired and weary. I can't sleep; I can't rest.
Even though I'm exhausted.
My mind races with worry and fear.
I feel trapped. Set me free, oh Lord.
Calm my heart.
Let me know that true rest is found in you alone.
Not in people, circumstances or worldly solutions.
Rest comes in learning to trust you.
Comfort me at night. Show me I can overcome my struggles by your strong and loving hand.
Guide my heart and my life.
Let me go deep into the truth.
I am forgiven. I am loved by Christ Jesus.
His love so sweet.
Let me rest and sleep deeply in the loving arms of my Savior.
In the name of Jesus,
Amen.

10 ANXIETY & WORRY

There is no fear in love, but perfect love casts out fear. For fear has to do with punishment, and he who fears is not perfected in love. We love, because he first loved us.

1 John 4:18-19

Dear loving Lord,
I am feeling stress. I am worried.
Too many things occupy my mind.
Won't you help me?
Show me Lord your order and
your plans are eternal.
Let me trust in your will alone.
Your Word tells me where there is love
there is no fear.
Your perfect love drives out all fear.
Let me be filled with your love.
The perfect love that tells me
I am not condemned.
Instead, I am saved.
I can do all things through you.
You strengthen me.
In the name of Christ Jesus,
Amen.

11 BE FULL OF THE SPIRIT

*...even the Spirit of truth, whom the world
cannot receive, because it neither sees him
nor knows him; you know him, for he dwells
with you, and will be in you.*

John 14:17

Oh loving Lord,
I come before you, I seek your presence,
As I'm empty without you.
So here and now, oh dear Lord,
I ask you to fill me.
Pour your Spirit into me.
I open up my heart and soul to your tender healing
and loving mercy.
Pour out your Spirit, oh Lord.
Free me, cleanse me, restore me.
Make me new again.
Let your grace work in me to build my strength
and to give me clarity.
Fill me with the peace of Christ.
Only in you can I receive true rest.
Only in you can my heart find heavenly joy.
Jesus won it all for me on the cross.
He is risen - and so am I - by your goodness alone.
Fill me Lord, may your Spirit live in me.
In Jesus' name,
Amen.

12 FREE & HEAL MY FAMILY

No one will be able to stand against you all the days of your life. As I was with Moses, so I will be with you; I will never leave you nor forsake you. Be strong and courageous, because you will lead these people to inherit the land I swore to their ancestors to give them.

Joshua 1:5-6

Dear heavenly Father,
Do you see us? Broken and imprisoned by selfishness, hurt & silence.
Won't you help us please?
Send your Spirit, oh Lord!
Forgive us! Save us! Pour out your mercy now!
Cast out the enemy!
Give me courage to continue in prayer and service.
No matter what it takes, no matter how long.
I know Christ fights for us. I know he died for us.
He rose again on the 3rd day.
May your truth reach even the hardest of hearts.
Set the captives free, wash our deepest wounds,
and let me not be hurried my Lord.
Teach me to wait upon your grace and rest in your will. My family is worth the wait.
Unite us in your all-consuming love.
In the holy name of Christ Jesus,
Amen.

13 HEAL A RELATIONSHIP

Above all hold unfailing your love for one another, since love covers a multitude of sins.

1 Peter 4:8

Dear beloved Lord,
We've been hurting too long, there's too much silence, too much pain.
Won't you help us? Won't you heal us?
Let me let go of trying to figure it all out.
Let me let go of who's right and who's wrong.
Instead, may I feel Christ embracing us.
Let us be better for each other.
Let us find a common ground where love
heals all wounds.
Soften my heart, oh Father.
Let me follow the example of your Son.
He does not seek control, but instead,
loving sacrifice.
This is the source of his glory,
born of mercy and trust in God almighty.
Let me trust you can heal.
Let me trust we can change.
Bring us to you, bring us together again.
I know by your sweet mercy,
All things are possible.
In the holy name of Jesus,
Amen.

14 STRENGTH IN TRIALS

All those gathered here will know that it is
not by sword or spear that the Lord saves;
for the battle is the Lord's, and he will give
all of you into our hands.

1 Samuel 47

Oh almighty Lord,
It's just too much sometimes.
Worry and fear crowd my life and my mind.
So many struggles at once.
What can I do my Lord?
The battle is in my mind. The enemy comes and
whispers in my ear the lie that all is lost.
Give me strength, oh Lord, to reject the enemy.
Let me look to Christ upon the cross for me,
glorified at your right hand,
sending me the power of his Holy Spirit.
Let me stand up for myself and say, "I can do this.
I can face the giant down; I can defeat him,
As the mighty hand of God is upon me."
May it glorify you, oh Lord,
and may the angels in heaven sing praises
at the sight of this sinner restored.
Glory to God in the highest!
In Jesus' name,
Amen.

15 FEEL LIKE GIVING UP

But they who wait for the Lord shall renew
their strength, they shall mount up with wings
like eagles, they shall run and not be weary,
they shall walk and not faint.

Isaiah 40:31

Dear loving Lord,
Everything is too hard for me right now.
I just want to give up.
Where are you Lord? Do you see me struggling?
Do you see me broken?
Lift me up, oh Lord!
Give me the strength to somehow raise my arms,
and lift up my voice to praise you.
Even though everything seems to be falling apart,
show me when I praise you, the walls come down,
the chains are broken, and the prisoners go free.
May my praise reveal your glory.
You alone are all powerful.
You alone can make this small child strong again.
Let me rest secure, in **Christ resurrected.**
I pray for this in Jesus' name,
Amen.

16 UNCERTAINTY

*May the God of peace himself sanctify you
wholly; and may your spirit and soul and
body be kept sound and blameless at the
coming of our Lord Jesus Christ.*

1 Thessalonians 5:23

Oh merciful Lord,
Things seem unclear. I'm not sure where I stand,
or if the decisions I make are correct.
Too many thoughts swirl around and confuse me.
The enemy brings uncertainty and fear to my heart.
Stand up for me, my Lord, fight for me!
Cast away the darkness. Show me your will.
Bring me clarity and peace.
Even if I can't have all the answers,
I know the One who does.
Your Spirit created the universe.
Your Spirit brought Jesus back to life.
Let your Spirit, my Lord, bring me certainty.
The certainty that you will never leave me.
You will always lead me,
and I belong to you.
In Jesus' name,
Amen.

17 NO MORE NEGATIVITY

When hard pressed, I cried to the LORD;
he brought me into a spacious place.

Psalm 118:23

Dear heavenly Father,
I feel the walls of my mind closing in upon me.
My head is filled with negativity.
Help me Father. Free me Lord from this prison of
negative thought.
I don't want to expect the worst from
situations or people.
I don't want to lose hope.
My wounds and my weakness limit me.
So I go to the only place where I have
a fighting chance.
In your presence, I begin to see the light.
In your Word, I find the Rock to grab hold of.
Cleanse me Lord.
Free my mind - as only you can.
Free my soul.
Let me be free to be me again Father,
filled with hope, alive in love.
In Jesus' name,
Amen.

18 WHEN YOU FEEL LIKE A FAILURE

*For I am convinced that neither death nor life,
neither angels nor demons, neither the present nor
the future, nor any powers, neither height nor
depth, nor anything else in all creation, will be able
to separate us from the love of God that is in Christ
Jesus our Lord.*

Romans 8:38-39

Dear loving Lord,
Is it over? Is it finished?
Have I come this far, only to fail?
I feel like nothing. Can you help me?
Give me the courage to see you again on the cross.
Broken, beaten, humiliated. Isn't that how I feel?
You went through death. You passed through.
And after 3 days the Spirit called you back.
Call to me Lord! Come to me!
Show my heart that no matter what I've done,
or didn't do -- I am still your child.
May your Spirit take hold of me.
Is anything greater than a lost soul lifting up their
voice in thanks and praise to almighty God?
So here I declare your victory over my failure
put to death on the cross.
Let me rise again with you.
Strong, complete, forgiven… and loved.
In the name of Jesus,
Amen.

19 I NEED JOY

*Therefore let us be grateful for receiving a
kingdom that cannot be shaken, and thus let
us offer to God acceptable worship, with
reverence and awe, for our God is a
consuming fire.*

Hebrews 12:28-29

Oh loving Father,
I've got my problems and my pain,
But the one thing I pray for is that your joy
never leaves me.
Let me remain joyous.
Your Spirit opens up the heavens to show me the
loving face of your Son Jesus.
He looks upon me with compassion and mercy.
He cries out to you, oh Father, on my behalf.
What more can I ask? What more can I desire?
The Son of God giving his all for me at all times?
Let this truth burst forth from the depth of my
soul to quiet my fears and soothe the hurt.
May the love of Christ consume me;
His eternal tenderness caressing my heart.
And let my response be joy.
Pure joy.
In Jesus' name I pray,
Amen.

20 KNOW JESUS

But to all who received him, who believed in his name, he gave power to become children of God; who were born, not of blood nor of the will of the flesh nor of the will of man, but of God. And the Word became flesh and dwelt among us, full of grace and truth; we have beheld his glory, glory as of the only Son from the Father.

John 1:12-14

Dear Jesus,
Who are you? Do I really know you?
Are you just a concept, a wise man from the past?
What does it mean, oh Lord, to truly know you?
Let me open myself, to take the risk and surrender.
If my heart is closed, I can never know anyone.
Let me know all the stories about you are true.
Your teaching, how you healed, when you cried
for your friends, the depth of your prayer,
how the whip cracked on your back,
and how much you bled for me.
Transform my heart to know your word is true and
you are faithful.
And yes, you came back for me –
back from the dead.
Let me know this was all for me,
Since you love me, and I am yours.
Let me know you, oh Jesus,
and love you as my Savior, my Lord.
In your holy name, Amen.

21 STAY FOCUSED ON GOD

*...so that you may live a life worthy of the
Lord and please him in every way: bearing
fruit in every good work, growing in the
knowledge of God*

Colossians 1:10

Dear merciful Lord,
In silence and prayer I feel your presence.
Yet back in the world I forget.
Why do I lose sight of you?
I know you, I trust you, but I get distracted and fail.
I let my flesh react without thinking or care,
ignoring or hurting others, even though
I don't want to. Won't you change me, oh Lord?
I can't do it on my own. Remove the hardness in
my heart that hides your grace.
When I arise from prayer
let me not forget your love.
May my prayer continue when I meet with people.
May your mercy go forth,
as I was saved by your mercy.
Let me stand firm on principles,
on the rock that is Christ. His Spirit gives me life.
Help me be humble, my Lord.
May your hand never leave me.
Let my life glorify you.
In Jesus' name,
Amen.

22 STRENGTH

Have I not commanded you? Be strong and
of good courage; be not frightened, neither
be dismayed; for the Lord your God is with
you wherever you go.

Joshua 1:9

Oh beloved God,
I am weak.
I have no strength in my hands.
My soul is tired. I hunger and thirst for you.
Help me please. Let me praise you.
Fill me with your Spirit. Give me strength.
I open my heart to you to see things clearly.
I see my weakness. This is truth. This is strength.
But you look with mercy,
upon the fragile and the broken.
Your loving mercy lifts me up to be filled
with your love.
Give strength to these dry bones.
Washed clean by Christ's blood,
I share in his victory over sin and death.
Let me be strong, dear Lord,
since Christ is strong in me.
In Jesus' name I pray,
Amen.

23 PANIC

*And he awoke and rebuked the wind, and said
to the sea, "Peace! Be still!" And the wind
ceased, and there was a great calm.*

Mark 4:39

Heavenly Father,
I am being attacked. Please help me. This is real.
A war rages against me and my soul.
My only way to fight is to cry out.
So I cry out to you, my Lord, my God!
Send legions of angels and
your Holy Spirit to defend me.
Right here. Right now.
You are all that is good. You are all that I need.
You are my peace and security. Jesus, I trust in you.
Rise up, oh mighty Lord!
Against all evil attacking me,
Defend me now!
For you are holy, you are truth.
All righteousness and glory are yours alone.
You won the victory for me on the cross,
You poured out your love for me.
Rising up you revealed your glory and power.
Oh, loving God! Oh, merciful Lord! Free me now!
I give myself up to your tender mercy,
Into your loving hands.
In Jesus' name,
Amen.

24 FOR A LOVED ONE WHO NEEDS MERCY

And the prayer offered in faith will make the
sick person well; the Lord will raise them
up. If they have sinned, they will be forgiven.

James 5:15

Oh loving Lord,
At this moment I kneel before you,
I have no right to question your will or your ways.
Still, out of love, I beg for your mercy.
Please look upon my loved one with
forgiveness and compassion.
Send your Spirit to protect and defend.
May your grace work in the soul of my loved one.
Pour out your mercy. Bring clarity and peace.
Let my loved one's spirit fly free in
the redemption of the soul.
Establish your holy Kingdom. Conquer the heart.
Only you can do this, oh Lord.
Let me be a simple instrument of kindness.
Not interfering with the great work of your Spirit.
May it be for your glory, according to your will,
all given by the blood of Christ.
In Jesus' name,
Amen.

25 FEELING MISUNDERSTOOD

Trust in the Lord with all your heart
and lean not on your own understanding;
in all your ways submit to him,
and he will make your paths straight.

Proverbs 3:5-6

Dear loving Father,
Why does it seem like they're so far away?
Why can't they understand me? Why the distance?
Oh loving Lord, I feel abandoned.
I seek rest for my weary heart.
So I go to you again to be filled with your Spirit,
the Spirit of Truth.
You open my mind and my heart. You tell me,
"Be quiet. Be still.
Let my work and my will be done.
Trust in me. Rest in me.
This way I will give you a humble, merciful heart.
Then you will learn to love as I love my Son,
and as my Son loves you."
Let it be this way, oh Lord!
Let your mighty grace break down the walls
that separate our love.
Bring us together in spirit and truth.
And let our understanding
give praise and glory to God.
In Jesus' name,
Amen.

26 FEEL YOU CAN'T GO ON

*Count it all joy, my brethren, when you
meet various trials, for you know that the
testing of your faith produces steadfastness.*

James 1:2-3

Oh loving Lord,
Sometimes I feel I just can't go on anymore.
The days and nights stretch far and long,
I yearn for rest, but I can't find any.
Can you hear me Lord? Are you there?
With my head I understand, but it's my heart that
bleeds from the weight of the day and the
burden of life.
Come to me, oh sweet Jesus.
Let me feel your presence.
Let me meditate upon the cross you embraced.
You are human. You felt how it hurts to be
frustrated and sad.
Jesus, only you know me completely.
Come to me Lord! Come to me now.
I seek you desperately. Your tender touch
and forgiving caress surely will heal my wounds.
Lift me up again. I trust only in you.
You are all I need.
In your precious name,
Sweet Jesus,
Amen.

27 TO GAIN INSIGHT

"You are the light of the world.... Let your
light so shine before men, that they may see
your good works and give glory to your
Father who is in heaven."

Matthew 5:14a,16

Dear loving God,
It seems like confusion and challenges never end.
How much longer Lord?
Here and now I seek clarity.
I seek the vision of God.
Help me accept my smallness in your infinite plan.
Your ways are higher than mine.
Your plan divine and eternal. What remains for me?
Let me see as Jesus sees.
Let me look beyond problems and see people
instead. Give me the insight to see through the
darkness illuminated by your Light.
The resurrection of Christ brings light to the world.
Let your light shine in me and from me.
Set me upon a high hill so I may see clearly.
May your goodness allow me to share your light
with others. Let it be brilliant for you.
All for your heavenly glory,
All for the Kingdom of God.
In Jesus' name,
Amen.

28 FEELING ALONE

It is the Lord who goes before you; he will be with you, he will not fail you or forsake you; do not fear or be dismayed.

Deuteronomy 31:8

Dear loving Father,
It seems as if I'm all alone.
I have no one to comfort me, no one to hold me.
Can I go to you? Will you embrace me?
My loneliness makes me feel so empty.
When Jesus felt alone he went to you, oh Lord.
He stretched out his arms, and cried out, "Father!"
So now, I go to him, the beloved Son of the Father.
Dear Jesus, take away my loneliness.
Let me feel you here with me.
Comfort me with your love.
With you I am never, ever alone.
You went to the cross for me.
You died for me.
And you live for me eternally.
You are forever faithful.
Let this truth fill my soul.
Let your love heal my heart.
And may my spirit soar with your Spirit
making all things new again.
Oh dearest Jesus, oh loving Christ!
You are my hope and my salvation.
In Jesus' name,
Amen.

29 ABSOLUTE PROTECTION

The Lord is my light and my salvation;
whom shall I fear?
The Lord is the stronghold of my life;
of whom shall I be afraid?

Psalm 27:1

Dear Almighty Father,
The enemy surrounds me, even my life is at risk.
So I look to the only place in the universe
where I have absolute protection.
In the House of the Lord.
In the fear of God I find wisdom.
Even if they destroy me, my soul is safe.
I live eternally only in you.
Eternal life begins today - with Christ - in me.
Fully protected by the pouring of your Holy Spirit
and your blood out upon me.
The enemy is crushed under your heel.
I invoke your protection in the holiest of names,
the name under which all must bow down.
In the name of
the Lord Jesus Christ,
Amen.

30 LOVE GOD FIRST

*Jesus answered, "The first is, 'Hear, O Israel: The Lord
our God, the Lord is one; and you shall love the Lord
your God with all your heart, and with all your soul, and
with all your mind, and with all your strength.' The
second is this, 'You shall love your neighbor as yourself.'
There is no other commandment greater than these."*
Mark 12:29-31

Dear heavenly Lord,
Let me love you above all things, above all people.
Let my heart seek you first as you are life –
you are love.
Let me not demand from anyone
what you alone can give me.
True confidence and peace come from you alone.
Let me not ask anyone to grant me the promises
that come only from your grace.
May my heart understand that in loving you first
I can love others more. For those that hunger and
thirst have nothing left to give.
Fill me with your Spirit, make my inner life
abundant, so I can love as you love;
giving my life and asking nothing in return.
Even though I failed and sinned
you called out to me; your goodness drew me in.
Let me love you first, oh Lord
Above all other things.
In Jesus' name,
Amen.

31 A FRESH START

Behold, I am doing a new thing;
  now it springs forth, do you not perceive it?
I will make a way in the wilderness
  and rivers in the desert.

Isaiah 43:19

Dear merciful Lord,
I trust you, I seek you. You are my Lord, my God.
At this time in my life I feel stuck.
I can't move forward.
Won't you bring to me the Good News once again?
Prepare me, oh Lord. Get me ready.
May your Spirit breathe renewal into me.
Let it happen according to your terms and timing.
Begin in me again, oh Lord.
Refresh and restore my faith.
God alone is the creator. You make all things new.
In the most humble place, a King is born.
After failure and disaster,
Christ walks the earth again.
Pour out your Spirit and truth to fill my thirsty soul.
May I rise up with my Lord
In blessed obedient love.
In Jesus' name,
Amen.

32 UNDER ATTACK

Hallelujah! Salvation and glory and power belong to
our God, for his judgments are true and just;
Hallelujah! For the Lord our God the Almighty reigns.
Let us rejoice and exult and give him the glory,

Revelation 19 (various)

Dear mighty Lord,
I am being attacked. Danger surrounds me.
So here and now I invoke your Spirit.
Defend me. Protect and cover me, oh Lord,
with the precious blood of Christ.
Send legions of angels to stand and fight for me.
Raise your mighty hand to cast out the enemy.
You have won the victory in my heart.
Now Lord, establish your victory in my life.
I trust only in you.
Show me my part in the fight.
Give me courage in Christ.
My greatest weapon is my praise to God.
May I join my voice with your heavenly choir
singing, Hallelujah!
The Lord of Hosts has won the victory.
Our Lord God Almighty reigns.
Let us rejoice and be glad.
Give him glory!
In Jesus' name,
Amen.

33 CHANGE OF HEART

*A new heart I will give you, and a new spirit
I will put within you; and I will take out of
your flesh the heart of stone and give you a
heart of flesh.*

Ezekiel 36:26

Dear loving God,
Thank you for another day of life.
Today I seek a change of heart.
I suffer from my hardness.
Please change me Lord. Only you can do this.
Give me a humble heart, a merciful heart.
Let me learn to trust you more and me less.
Let me understand, you alone are worthy.
You alone are the Lord,
and only by Christ's blood am I justified.
All my other efforts are but filthy rags when
compared to the great love you pour out upon me.
Change my heart God!
Cleanse me!
Soften my hardness. Forgive my sin. Let me be
tender and loving as you are to me.
In the sweet name of Jesus Christ,
Amen.

34 WHEN YOU HAVE TO WAIT

*Truly, truly, I say to you, you will weep and
lament, but the world will rejoice; you will be
sorrowful, but your sorrow will turn into joy.*

John 16:20

Dear heavenly Lord,
The world demands results,
and my own flesh seeks action.
Help me Lord, in this time of waiting.
No matter what happens,
no matter how things turn out,
may your Spirit remind me I already have all I need.
Calm my fears and anxieties. Let me rest in you.
I am your child. You save my soul.
You give me life everlasting.
Let me be patient and still in your presence.
And during this time of wait, build my faith.
Strengthen my character. Reveal to my heart
how much I truly depend upon you.
So whatever may come, I'm ready,
to keep praising you, to glorify you,
and to serve you obediently.
Show me waiting for you is loving you.
You alone are my hope and salvation.
In Jesus' name, I pray,
Amen.

35 PEACE IN MY HEART

But now in Christ Jesus you who once were far off have been brought near in the blood of Christ.

Ephesians 2:13

Dear heavenly Lord,
I just can't get rid of the uneasiness
I feel in my heart.
Fear and worry choke me and make
my chest feel tight.
So I come to you now as I know only you,
can give me peace.
Not the peace that the world offers,
but the true peace of God,
not depending on circumstances or people,
or even myself.
But a peace that comes from the Prince of Peace,
the King of kings, the Lord of lords.
Jesus is my peace.
Only through him am I at rest with God.
Bring down the walls between us.
Let repentance set me free.
Unite me to you, oh sweet Jesus.
Preach your peace to me, oh Lord.
Bring comfort to my heart.
In Jesus' holy name,
Amen.

36 A NEW BEGINNNING

For our God is a consuming fire.

Hebrews 12:29

Dear heavenly Father,
I'm tired and weary, my body and heart heavy,
from hurting for so long.
Is it possible to start anew?
Can you send your Spirit to lift me up again?
All suffering and pain, all betrayal and failure,
none of this compares to the love of Christ.
My past does not define me,
as his love burns it in an all-consuming fire.
So here and now I place it all
in his wounded side.
Oh dear Lord, let me begin again!
As a new person, forgiven and loved.
Born again, I am God's child.
All of this thanks to you.
All of this to glorify the Son.
All of this, for you are holy Lord,
Oh how great is your love!
In Jesus' name,
Amen.

37 FREEDOM FROM PAIN & SICKNESS

But he was wounded for our transgressions,
he was bruised for our iniquities;
upon him was the chastisement that made us whole,
and with his stripes we are healed.

Isaiah 53:5

Dear blessed Lord,
I don't want to complain, I know others suffer too,
but I really need you now.
Oh Jesus, you are the Great Physician,
I seek your healing touch. Reach out over me.
Send your Spirit to heal me.
Lift up my natural defenses.
Relieve my pain, restore my health.
And above all else, oh Lord, heal my soul.
Lift me up inside knowing
that no matter what happens
I am your child, I am your beloved.
My place in your heart is secure.
All this thanks to the Lamb of God
who suffered taking away the sins of the world.
Christ heals all wounds, he relieves all pain,
and dries my tears.
You are my restoration, dear Lord.
You are my salvation.
Free me from sickness and pain,
By the grace and mercy of almighty God.
In Jesus' name, Amen.

38 ACCEPT WHAT I CAN'T CHANGE

> *Jesus said to him, "I am the way, the truth, and the life. No one comes to the Father except through Me."*
>
> **John 14:6**

Oh heavenly Lord,
Is this what you want?
Is it right? Is it fair? How can this be?
My flesh and my fears rage against reality.
Help me, oh Lord, to hear your voice.
Help me understand.
Show me that you are in control of all things,
no matter how confusing or painful they may be.
I don't have to like it, but help me accept it.
Show me how to wait.
Close the doors that lead to resentment and anger.
Let me see the big picture. Show me, oh Lord.
True peace only comes from
the wounds of Christ.
You are my rest. You are my home.
When I accept you, I accept all that is your will.
Let your truth calm my heart and soothe my soul.
In Jesus' name,
Amen.

39 DO THE RIGHT THING

I am the vine; you are the branches. If you
remain in me and I in you, you will bear much
fruit; apart from me you can do nothing.
John 15:5

Dear loving Lord,
Why is everything so complicated?
Am I doing the right thing?
Righteousness and justice
are the foundation of your throne.
You are the Way, the Truth and the Life.
May your Word sink into my heart
And take possession of my soul.
Let me place your will above all other things.
Establish your Kingdom inside me, then extend it
to the rest of my life.
Let me remember that outside of your will
I can do nothing.
If I abide in you, my life brings forth great fruit.
Let it be this way for me, oh Lord.
Take control. Show me your will, and let me rest
in humble obedience.
This is God's will:
See Christ. Believe in him.
Have everlasting life. Be resurrected.
According to your will and your way,
All for your glory alone.
In Jesus' name,
Amen.

40 PERSEVERANCE

For still the vision awaits its time;
* it hastens to the end—it will not lie.*
If it seem slow, wait for it;
* it will surely come, it will not delay.*

Habakkuk 2:3

Dear loving Lord,
How long has it been?
How long have I asked and pleaded?
It's been years Lord.
Have you heard me pour out my soul before you?
Certainly you see me here again on my knees.
Let me trust in you, oh Lord.
Give me the will to keep asking and waiting –
come what may – for your mighty Spirit to act.
Show my heart, oh Lord, that my prayers
are not for nothing.
Each one another brick
to raise your Kingdom up high.
No matter how long it takes,
no matter how many prayers,
let me continue in Faith, Hope and Love.
As I know you love me, as Christ strengthens me,
I can do all things.
Praise and glory to God!
In the name of Christ Jesus,
Amen.

41 DEEPEST PRAISE

Beloved, let us love one another; for love is of God, and he who loves is born of God and knows God. He who does not love does not know God; for God is love.

1 John 4:7

Dear loving Lord,
I'm a thief of your goodness.
I take advantage of your infinite love.
You give and you gave to me for oh so long,
especially in times of hurt and sorrow.
Without you, by now I'd be long gone.
Even when I sin or shut you out, you still let me
steal from your mercy. How can I understand such
unconditional love?
You love me at all costs.
God is love, God is love.
GOD IS LOVE!
Let my heart and my voice shout from the highest
mountain for all to hear the good news and rejoice!
There is no greater truth than the love poured out
over all humankind through my Savior Jesus Christ.
May his name alone be exalted,
above all the nations,
and over God's great creation.
In Jesus' name,
Amen.

42 THE IMPOSSIBLE

All these things my hand has made,
and so all these things are mine,
says the Lord.
But this is the man to whom I will look,
he that is humble and contrite in spirit,
and trembles at my word.

Isaiah 66:2

Dear loving Lord,
For you all things are possible.
So I come before you to seek the impossible.
Is there anything beyond your power and might?
Show me first, oh Lord,
if what I ask benefits my soul and your Kingdom.
Reveal to me what you desire.
Then, if you so choose, give me your Word.
Let it penetrate my heart.
Let me trust that you are in control.
May I seek your presence in prayer and fasting
to witness the impossible.
Cast away my doubt. Remove my fears.
Let your faithfulness shine inside me.
By your will and your way may it be done.
Let your promise burn deep in my soul,
no matter what it takes.
May it nourish my confidence in Christ alone.
In the name of Jesus,
Amen.

43 DECISION MAKING

Make me to know thy ways, O Lord;
teach me thy paths.
Lead me in thy truth, and teach me,
for thou art the God of my salvation;
for thee I wait all the day long.

Psalm 25:4-5

Oh heavenly Father,
I face a decision and don't know what to do.
I'm not at peace. Bring me your peace.
The peace of your Spirit, the peace of God.
First of all calm me. Let me know again
you are in control of all things.
Give me discernment. Give me clarity.
Do not let circumstances or my insecurity
get in the way of your will.
Let me see things as you see them.
Make it so that I don't even have to decide.
Only receive your Word and obey.
In this way I imitate Christ,
your beloved Son, my Savior and Lord.
Let your will be done in this decision
and in my life.
In Jesus' name,
Amen.

44 A LOVED ONE THAT HURTS YOU

And now these three remain: faith, hope and love. But the greatest of these is love.

1 Corinthians 13:13

Dear loving Lord,
I come to you wounded and tired from fighting
too long. Give me rest, oh Lord.
My loved one hurts me. I don't know
what to do. How much more I can stand?
Won't you help me, dear Lord?
Pour out your Spirit upon us.
Pour out your blood, pour out your love.
Free us from the enemy that seeks to divide us.
Only you can set us free.
Change me first Father. Fill my heart.
So when my loved one comes to me to hurt or
accuse, the only thing I offer is the love of
Christ in my heart.
Rise up, oh Lord!
Defend us from the evil one!
Extend your mighty hand and free us now!
Heal our hearts, oh Lord.
Heal the wounds between us. Show us how.
I seek the sweet pasture of your restoration.
By your will and your way. All glory to you.
In the name of Jesus,
Amen.

45 FOCUS

May your deeds be shown to your servants,
your splendor to their children.
May the favor of the Lord our God rest on us;
establish the work of our hands for us—
yes, establish the work of our hands.

Psalm 90:16-17

Dear holy Lord,
Too many things call for my attention.
Chores and responsibilities pile up a mile high.
It's all too much for me… but not for you.
May your mighty Spirit work in me.
Help me focus, oh Lord,
Give me clarity and direction. Pull me together.
Unite my mind, heart and body to finish the task.
Your hand upon me makes me quick, nimble and
efficient. I do not stray.
Where I can't make it, your Spirit fills in the gaps.
Cover me with your grace. I trust in you.
Calm my worry, cast out fear, and let me be certain
of your mighty will working in my life.
Let me do it for love, oh Lord,
for the love of my Savior, Christ Jesus,
In his holy name I pray,
Amen.

46 TEMPTATION

No temptation has overtaken you that is not
common to man. God is faithful, and he will not
let you be tempted beyond your strength, but
with the temptation will also provide the way of
escape, that you may be able to endure it.

1 Corinthians 10:13

Dear Heavenly Father,
You know my heart. You know I stumble
and sometimes fall. Right now I need you
for I am being tempted.
Won't you help me, oh Lord?
I admit my weakness and vulnerability.
Before you I am broken.
Only you can strengthen me to face the enemy
that offers me false promises and lies.
I am tempted and weak, but in Christ I find victory.
Rise up, oh mighty Lord!
Strike down the evil one. Expel him into the abyss.
May your Spirit fight for me.
Make my character firm and strong.
With my eyes fixed on Jesus no temptation will
overcome me.
The secret is your mercy. There I find peace,
There I find rest. It's the safest place I know.
Accept my prayer, oh holy Father,
In the name of your beloved Son,
Jesus Christ,
Amen.

47 DISAPPOINTED

For my thoughts are not your thoughts,
neither are your ways my ways, says the Lord.
For as the heavens are higher than the earth,
so are my ways higher than your ways
and my thoughts than your thoughts.

Isaiah 55:8-9

Oh merciful God,
I did not expect this. I hoped for something else.
I'm left without peace. How did this happen? Why?
Let me know all understanding and wisdom
are found in your forgiving wounds.
Give me a heart full of humility, mercy,
and trust in the Lord.
Let me know every failure is infinitely greater than
any victory when your will is done.
Show me what I must learn.
Help me trust in you.
You alone are my rest.
You alone are my hope.
You alone are my glory.
In Jesus' name,
Amen.

48 TO FORGIVE

...and be kind to one another, tenderhearted,
forgiving one another, as God in Christ
forgave you.

Ephesians 4:32

Oh merciful Lord,
Your word tells me, and I know I should forgive.
I struggle with this. The pain too deep.
You know how much it hurt to be betrayed.
Your heart pierced by actions you never asked for.
So you went to your Father.
Take me, oh Lord, with you to his loving arms.
Let my soul receive your grace that tells me
I too have been forgiven of much.
May your Spirit guide my heart and mind to forgive.
I may not like it, I may not forget,
but I can decide.
I can choose to forgive. I can choose to love.
Pour yourself out over me.
Give my heart rest, oh Lord.
As your mercy flows through me and from me.
Make it so, my loving Savior, Lamb of God.
You take away the sins of the world.
In Jesus' name,
Amen.

49 THANK YOU JESUS

For God so loved the world that he gave his only Son, that whoever believes in him should not perish but have eternal life.

John 3:16

Oh sweet Jesus,
You did so much for me, but you didn't have to.
You could have said, "No, I won't."
You could have saved yourself,
but instead you saved me.
You could have went on being God's Son,
but instead you brought me into the presence of
your Father so I could be his child too.
Nothing could have been harder than to
receive the whip and hang upon that cross
for my sins.
So easy for me, so hard for you.
The only explanation
is love.
Thank you Jesus for letting this tired, weary and
wretched soul rise up clean and glorious with you.
Only you.
In Jesus' name,
Amen.

ABOUT THE AUTHOR

Vincent H Chough brings inspiration to thousands of readers every month through his books and web page PrayerForAnxiety.com. For over a decade, Vince has helped coordinate Bible study groups throughout northern Buenos Aires. This includes hard to reach places such as prisons and poor neighborhoods - he is witness to the tremendous healing power of God's Word. Vince also dedicates his time to discipleship in schools and communities.

PrayerForAnxiety.com offers prayers and insight to people from over 195 countries across the world. Vincent earned his medical degree at the University of Pittsburgh Medical Center and practiced medicine in the USA for 10 years. He now lives in Argentina with his wife and five children.

ALSO BY THE AUTHOR

Be With Him, Be Like Him

by Vincent H Chough

Looking for a change? Pray for it!

Clear and straightforward ways to change your life through prayer.

Discover life changing perspectives in *Be With Him, Be Like Him*. Begin your transforming journey today. Available at Amazon now.

Made in the USA
Coppell, TX
15 February 2023

12872843R00038